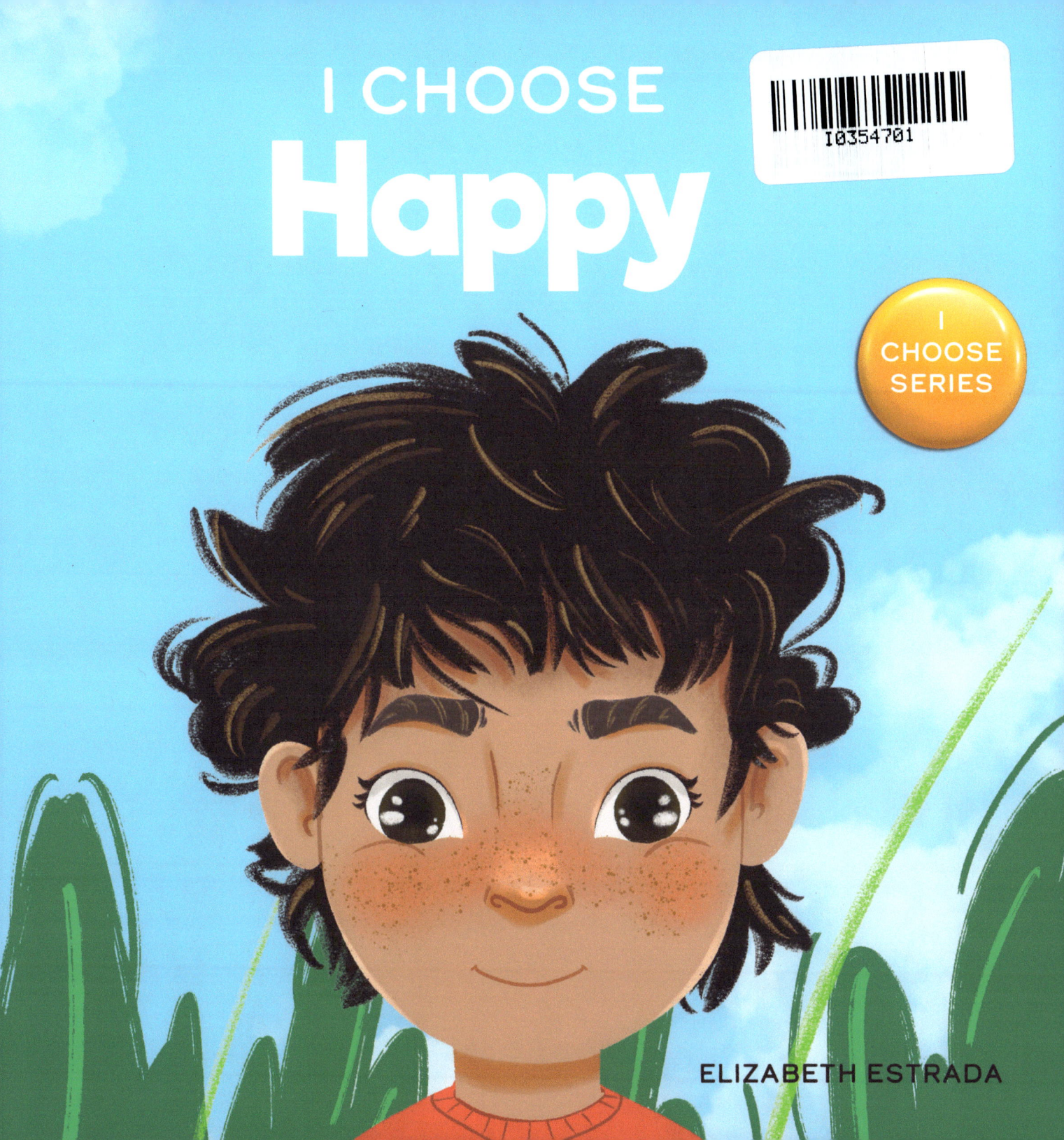

Copyright 2021 by Elizabeth Estrada - All rights reserved.
Published and printed in the USA.

No part of this publication or the information in it may be quoted or
reproduced in any form by means of printing, scanning, photocopying,
or otherwise without permission of the copyright holder.

I CHOOSE
Happy

ELIZABETH ESTRADA

DEDICATED TO MY MOTHER AND FATHER.

I was negative and miserable
And not a lot of **fun**.
It was like a cloud was overhead
Blocking out the **sun**.

I'd heard my face was nice
With a really lovely **smile**.
But I hadn't shown the world
My teeth for quite a **while**.

I never told a joke
And often wore a **frown**.
So many things in life
Just seemed to get me **down**.

I'd stand before the mirror
In my bedroom every **night**
And didn't see what others saw.
I couldn't see the **light**.

I didn't like my nose,
My mouth, or my **hair**.
I didn't like my sneakers
Or the clothes I had to **wear**.

I didn't feel very smart
Like all the **rest**.
"I'm bound to fail,"
I'd say before a **test**.

When chosen for the soccer team,
I'd say, "There's no **denying**.
We're going to lose for sure.
So what's the point of **trying**?"

I never paid a compliment
To anyone at **all**.
It was hard for me
To stand **tall**.

My parents tried their best
To lift the doom and **gloom**,
But all I did was shut my door
And mope around in my **room**.

All this negativity just
Simply wasn't **cool**,
And made me quite sad
And mopey at **school**.

"Try optimism, Luke,"
And hope for the **best**.
"When you are positive,
It helps you to feel **blessed**.

When I looked up the word - optimism,
It means you think positive and **bright**.
You're full of hope
And believe that things will be all **right**.

I went to bed and in my head,
I couldn't **disagree**.
A more positive and optimistic person
Was what I wanted to **be**.

I've spent too long
Being miserable and **blue**.
I can change my outlook.
Happiness can be mine, **too**!

I got up in the morning
With a hopeful **heart**,
And dressed in sunny colors
For a positive **start**.

I was nervous and excited,
And of course, I had my **doubts**.
"Just don't give up," I told myself.
"You have to tough it **out**."

At school, I said, "Hello"
To all the kids I **knew**,
And shared a smile with everyone.
It didn't matter **who**.

I gave nice compliments,
And I even **volunteered**.
I felt enthusiastic which
I hadn't felt for **years**.

I didn't even stumble
When I had to take a **test**.
"You can do this," I told myself.
"Just try to do your **best**."

I took the field for soccer,
Fit and ready to **begin**.
"Come on," I said to everyone.
"Let's go get that **win**."

I didn't always get things right,
But gave myself a **break**.
"You'll get there eventually.
Just learn from your **mistakes**."

I changed my ways
And my **mood**,
By looking on the bright side
With a better **attitude**.

So negative me was no more,
And everyone **agreed**,
I was now the kind of person
Who was more likely to **succeed**.

By choosing happiness,
I became a different **person**.
I am happier and more positive.
Success will be mine, for **certain**!

Download your free pdf of Positive Affirmations for Kids today at www.ichoosebooks.com

1. There is no one better to be than myself.
2. I am enough.
3. I get better every single day.
4. I am an amazing person.
5. All of my problems have solutions.
6. Today I am a leader.
7. I forgive myself for my mistakes.
8. My challenges help me grow.
9. I am perfect just the way I am.
10. My mistakes help me learn and grow.
11. Today is going to be a great day.
12. I have courage and confidence.
13. I can control my own happiness.
14. I have people who love and respect me.
15. I stand up for what I believe in.
16. I believe in my goals and dreams.
17. It's okay not to know everything.
18. Today I choose to think positive.
19. I can get through anything.
20. I can do anything I put my mind to.
21. I give myself permission to make choices.
22. I can do better next time.

23. I have everything I need right now.
24. I am capable of so much.
25. Everything will be okay.
26. I believe in myself.
27. I am proud of myself.
28. I deserve to be happy.
29. I am free to make my own choices.
30. I deserve to be loved.
31. I can make a difference.
32. Today I choose to be confident.
33. I am in charge of my life.
34. I have the power to make my dreams true.
35. I believe in myself and my abilities.
36. Good things are going to come to me.
37. I matter.
38. My confidence grows when I step outside of my comfort zone.
39. My positive thoughts create positive feelings.
40. Today I will walk through my fears.
41. I am open and ready to learn.
42. Every day is a fresh start.
43. If I fall, I will get back up again.
44. I am whole.
45. I only compare myself to myself.
46. I can do anything.
47. It is enough to do my best.
48. I can be anything I want to be.
49. I accept who I am.
50. Today is going to be an awesome day.

Dear Reader,

Thank you to my readers. I hope you enjoyed "I Choose Happy." I spent a lot of time developing this book and series.

So please tell me what you liked and even what you disliked. What kind of emotion should be in my next book?

I love to receive messages from my readers. Please write to me at Elizabethestradainfo@gmail.com

I would also greatly appreciate it if you could review my book. Your feedback matters a lot to me!

With love,
Elizabeth

www.ingramcontent.com/pod-product-compliance
Lightning Source LLC
Chambersburg PA
CBHW041521070526
44585CB00002B/40